This book comes to you,

_____,
(name)

on the occasion of

_____.
(celebrated event and date)

May you always find your way to a happy heart.

With love,

_____

Always and Never

20 TRUTHS FOR A HAPPY HEART

LISA SHUMATE

LUCIDBOOKS

Always and Never™
20 Truths for a Happy Heart

Copyright © 2019 by Lisa Shumate

Published by Lucid Books in Houston, TX
www.LucidBooksPublishing.com

eISBN-10: 1-63296-285-3
eISBN-13: 978-1-63296-285-0
ISBN-10: 1-63296-321-3
ISBN-13: 978-1-63296-321-5

Special Sales: Most Lucid Books titles are available in special quantity discounts. Custom imprinting or excerpting can also be done to fit special needs. Contact Lucid Books at Info@LucidBooksPublishing.com.

I'm deeply grateful to my family for their unconditional love, support, and inspiration.

My mother, the ultimate role model in strength and resilience.

My dad, who always saw the good in everyone.

My grandmother, who freely shared her wisdom and kind spirit.

My siblings—Gina, Sal, and Toni—because whenever we're together, there is always laughter.

And my husband, Chris, our children, William and Caroline, daughter-in-law Jacqueline, and grandson, Luke—you're my constant source of joy, sense of home, and a happy, happy heart!

To Alex, Ashton, and all the other young men and women moving into adulthood—this is for you.

Contents

Special thanks to the supportive and talented team at Lucid Books. I look forward to continued collaboration in the pursuit of sharing words that heal, guide, and inspire.

Foreword

We live in complicated times. As the world seems to move faster, grow less certain, and feel more divided and dangerous, it's all too easy to lose touch with ourselves and with the simpler aspects of our lives.

Which is why I am so honored to be writing this foreword.

I crossed paths with Lisa many years ago. In truth, I don't recall where. But I do recall her. I recall her energy. I recall her big heart. And I recall her passion for people. Back then, I was just starting out on a brand-new path, in a big new country, in the home of the brave. Every word of encouragement made a whole world of difference to my own bravery. Lisa had many such words.

Wind the clock forward a decade or more, and it is easy to reminisce longingly for what felt like simpler times. Times when we could not imagine the kind of dehumanizing rhetoric and divisiveness that dominates our headlines today. Yet here we are.

Which begs the question, how do we navigate our daily lives amid this brave new world in which so much of what we once took for granted is no more? By returning to the universal and timeless principles that transcend our differences and pull us through the fear and furor—back toward the truth of our hearts and the sacredness of our shared humanity.

Lisa shares those truths in this book. Its simplicity belies its potency. It reminds us that we alone are responsible for the state of our hearts and the shape of our lives—that no matter what is going on around us, within us lies the power to choose how we will respond.

Life is a gift. This book is a gift. It is no coincidence this book has found its way into your hands at this precise moment. Turn its pages and see what speaks to you. Something will. And whatever that is, it will nudge you in a direction that will help you become more of the person God created you to be. Don't miss that opportunity. Rather, seize it with an open mind and brave heart. What you yearn for most in the world will require no less.

—Margie Warrell,
International keynote speaker,
Bestselling author of *Find Your Courage and Stop Playing Safe*

Introduction

There are moments in our lives that usher in transition. They can catch us off guard or be marked with ceremony and celebration. From graduate to employee, old job to new job, single to married to single again, and so on. These moments can be heartbreaking or exhilarating and almost always throw open the door to uncertainty.

I wrote this book to be your constant companion—whether used to find firm footing when the ground seems shaky or for inspiration to set your outlook for a busy day. When you embrace *Always* and *Never* as mantras, you are reaching for your better self. You are rising above what is likely a temporary roadblock or challenge. You are marshalling a greater power of awareness and in so doing pivoting from reactive to mindful. When in a mindful state, you establish through action what defines your important relationships: trust, gratitude, boundaries, self-respect, and respect for others. I believe *Always* and *Never* play an important role in individual fulfillment and are especially comforting when you feel disappointed by people or a turn of events.

On a larger scale, *Always* and *Never* are guardrails for the ideals and standards we hold dear. They frame the kind of world we want for ourselves and our children.

Always and *Never* have the capacity to enable a quiet mind, peaceful spirit, and happy heart. Why is this notion of a happy heart so important? The happy heart has a unique, universal purpose in perpetual demand—the herculean might and humane calling to lift up others.

Truth #1

ALWAYS

be in charge of your thoughts.

What you say and how you feel start with the way you think. The way you think about everything is in your control. Thoughts are like seeds that need to be watered and nurtured with real knowledge, by real experts and real friends. A curious, open mind lets in the necessary sunshine.

NEVER

forget that you are in charge of the way you think and that a healthy mind requires ongoing fertilization.

Truth #2

ALWAYS

listen before speaking.

And then listen some more. Listen to understand, to demonstrate empathy, and to give the gift of your time and attention. Listen with your eyes as well as your ears. This requires slowing down long enough to truly see the person in front of you. When people want to talk, especially loved ones, they're rarely seeking answers from you. They want a sounding board, reassurance, and to connect with someone close to them.

NEVER

dominate conversation—you have two ears and one mouth for a reason.

Truth #3

ALWAYS
follow the Golden Rule.

Buddhism, Christianity, Confucianism, Hinduism, Islam, and Judaism all subscribe to a version of the Golden Rule in their religious teachings. It's a simple notion that has endured through the ages: Treat others the way you'd like to be treated. Kindness, patience, and being first to say "I'm sorry" are the hallmarks of the Golden Rule, and the rewards to you are long-lasting: inner peace and a life of no regret.

NEVER

let the mean acts of others cause you to break the Golden Rule.

Truth #4

ALWAYS
tell the truth.

Be honest with yourself and with others, and you will set the standard for truth in all situations. The truth keeps your conscience clear and intentions transparent. Only speak about what you know to be fact. Don't spread rumors, half-truths, or any information that may be inaccurate. Make sure you know the facts and sources of information before sharing.

NEVER

gossip or waste time with those who do.

Truth #5

ALWAYS

do as you say you will.

Make your commitments a priority, and you'll earn something invaluable: trust. The ability to build and keep trust is worth more than anything else you can bring to the table. No skill, degree, or talent can replace reliability. Trust is the connective tissue between you and every important relationship in your life, including your parents, spouse, boss, coworkers, and friends.

NEVER

undermine the trust others place in you by not keeping your word.

Truth #6

ALWAYS
place a high value on you.

The most important relationship you will ever have is the one you have with yourself. Take care of your health on a daily basis. Follow your instincts and listen to your voice above all. Give yourself enough runway and second chances to realize your hopes and dreams. The compelling force for happiness and success in your life is you and only you.

NEVER

allow others to determine your ability and potential.

Truth #7

ALWAYS

be a student.

George Bernard Shaw is often credited with the adage, "Youth is wasted on the young." Wouldn't it be great to preserve all the wonders of youth as we gain the wisdom and knowledge that come long after high school and college? But there is something you can do to maintain your youthful outlook on life: always be a student. Seek out opportunities where you aren't the smartest person in the room. Read books and magazines that broaden your horizons. Continuing your education in formal and informal ways will keep you young and interesting.

NEVER

think you're too smart or too old to learn something new.

Truth #8

ALWAYS

separate opinion from fact.

Opinions are just that—one person's view. They can be wrapped in fear or prejudice. Opinions can make people as impervious as steel, preventing the passage to clear thinking or new possibilities. Keep your mind free of opinions and focus on acquiring real knowledge. Be wary of people who hold themselves as experts. The best knowledge possible is that which comes from your firsthand research and experiences. Get the facts before you make big purchases, cast your vote, or try to influence others.

NEVER

mistake opinion for fact.

Truth #9

ALWAYS
see the beauty in mistakes.

Allow yourself to see mistakes in a whole new light. Learn from them, and one day your mistakes will provide material for the stories you tell and heartfelt advice to others. Each time you make a mistake, you have the opportunity to learn from it, which will then build your self-confidence. Always forgive yourself and others for making mistakes. Make decisions based on the best information you have, and be confident you will be able to handle the outcome.

NEVER

allow mistakes to cause embarrassment or prevent you from trying again.

Truth #10

ALWAYS

share credit for success.

If you want to be known as a team player, to be included in big projects, and to be considered for promotion, look for ways to acknowledge others and their contributions. In fact, the group is always smarter than any one person, so why not make use of the group and give them their due credit? When you make coworkers feel part of something, they are inspired to do their best. People who inspire are literally pushed up the ladder by their peers.

NEVER

allow your desire for praise to overrule recognition for the group.

Truth #11

ALWAYS

embrace the rules.

Every company and every person have a set of rules that, when broken, violate trust. At work, rules apply to things such as dress code, schedules, expense reports, and the like. As individuals, our rules vary greatly. Don't assume you know what they are without asking. The rules that make me happy are being clutter-free and closely guarding family time and traditions. Embrace the rules of people you love and expect the same in return.

NEVER

think rules don't or shouldn't apply to you.

Truth #12

ALWAYS

choose financial security over money.

Financial security is not the same as money or salary. Financial security is what happens when you can sacrifice spending today to start saving for tomorrow. Set up a budget that keeps you in control of money instead of allowing money to control you. There's nothing you can buy today that you'll love as much as six figures in your bank account 10 years from now. Find ways to have fun today that allow you to save for tomorrow. Plan for a long future with yourself by building financial security one paycheck at time.

NEVER

depend on others for financial security.

Truth #13

ALWAYS

make time your friend.

Time can be your friend or your enemy. Make it your friend by developing habits that lead to health and well-being. Approach each day with a mix of planned activities and room for spontaneous opportunities. If you allow yourself to be overscheduled, you'll become resentful and fatigued. Preserve time for yourself to relax, reflect, and recharge. Time doesn't happen to you—it's a gift. What will you do with your gift today?

NEVER

live today wishing for tomorrow; embrace the present.

Truth #14

ALWAYS
find a way to forgive.

Forgiveness is one of the best things you can do to restore your own sense of peace and calm. When you accept this reality and live it, you'll free yourself of emotional baggage weighing you down. This is especially true when the one you most need to forgive is you. Forgiveness doesn't require you to change your mind about a relationship or boundaries. Forgiveness does require you to release sabotaging anger and hostility. In words that have been so famously sung in *Frozen*, "Let it go!"

NEVER

underestimate the benefits of forgiveness.

Truth #15

ALWAYS

keep the faith.

There will be times when faith will be the most important
ALWAYS. When you feel lonely or face difficulty that seems
to have no end, keep the faith that there will be better days.
Complete trust and confidence in a higher power working on
your behalf is well-placed energy. Spirituality, meditation, and
prayer will give you peace and perspective not easily obtained
from any other source.

NEVER

let anything come between you and your faith in tomorrow.

Truth #16

ALWAYS

love unconditionally.

There is no other way to love. If there are conditions or strings attached to your love for someone or to their love for you, it no longer qualifies as love. Before you commit to marriage or living with your significant other, be certain that unconditional love is a two-way street. Unconditional love doesn't mean unconditional access. Boundaries, time for yourself, and the understanding that you both will have other important loving relationships are part of the unconditional love equation. Unconditional love is not a blanket statement—it's an everyday practice. Every day.

NEVER

lose your sense of self in the pursuit of unconditional love.

Truth #17

ALWAYS

express gratitude.

It's not enough to be grateful—it's important to express your sincere thanks out loud and in writing. When others complain, be the one who finds the good in the situation. Being grateful is a habit, so is being a complainer. There is happiness and truth in gratitude. Practice it loudly and often.

NEVER

let negativity have the last word.

Truth #18

ALWAYS

anchor your dreams to achievement.

Dreaming is a verb that results in no action. *Achievement* is the word that builds careers. Think and plan in terms of achievement. Graduating with a strong GPA. Starting that creative project. Being the kind of person who goes above and beyond every day. Set goals and do what it takes to meet or exceed them. That's the way dreams come true.

NEVER

let your dreams be carried away by tides of inaction.

Truth #19

ALWAYS

preserve the beauty around you.

Nature doesn't belong to us—we're the caretakers for the next generation. Our lakes and parks are protected by laws about littering, but too many people are breaking those laws. Don't be one of them. Recycle and be mindful of how your habits are impacting the environment.

NEVER

neglect your duty to nature and the next generation.

Truth #20

ALWAYS

be the leader of your life.

Be intentional about the kind of journey you wish to take. Aim high. Don't waiver on your commitment or retreat from challenges. Aim high and stretch your capacity to learn and grow. Why do some people assume they aren't ready to lead? Every day, talented individuals see what they don't have in experience, skill, or credentials instead of seeing all they do have to offer. The difference between the candidate who thinks she is capable of moving up versus the one who thinks she doesn't have what it takes is the willingness to make the leap. Be the leader in knowing what you're trying to do and when you're ready to do it. Push, reach, persevere.

Truly leading your life also leads to a happy heart.

NEVER

minimize your potential or capacity to lead.

Conclusion

This book has come to you as a loving reminder, a moment of reassurance and reaffirmation of all that is important today and for the rest of your life. It comes from someone who has learned these timeless concepts the hard way—through experience.

I hope you share this little book with those you love. I hope it brings you comfort, joy, and all the blessings of a life well-lived.

Acknowledgments

This book is the culmination of many years of learning and leading from peers, teachers, friends, bosses, my university, my community, and national leaders.

I was empowered while attending Archbishop Chapelle, an all-girls high school in Metairie, Louisiana, where we students were in charge of everything—holding class offices, running the newspaper, serving as captains of the dance and drill team, and more. Simply put, girls ruled! Those memories will stay with me forever.

At Loyola University and WWL-TV in New Orleans, I stepped into my dream of working in television, while simultaneously receiving on-the-job training and a Bachelor of Arts in Communications.

My managers at Disney|ABC and TEGNA provided me the opportunity to develop business and community leadership skills.

As Associate Vice President and General Manager of Houston Public Media, the PBS and NPR stations for Houston, we're proud members of the University of Houston Cougar family.

The programming and people of PBS and NPR, along with the staff and faculty of the University of Houston, have shaped and stretched my thinking.

The men and women of Houston Public Media, backed by the Houston Public Media Foundation Board, believe media must live up to its potential to expand minds and possibilities. It's rewarding to work with you every day.

About the Author

Lisa Trapani Shumate is Associate Vice President of the University of Houston System and General Manager of Houston Public Media, and also serves as Executive Director of the Houston Public Media Foundation. She holds national leadership roles with PBS and the Public Television Major Market Group Board.

Lisa has more than 20 years of media management experience, is the recipient of numerous awards, and participated in an International Business Residency in China. She holds a Bachelor of Arts in Communications from Loyola University in New Orleans, Louisiana, and a Master of Business Administration from the University of Houston.

Lisa is expanding her media footprint to publishing with the goal of sharing wisdom and encouragement with young men and women entering adulthood.

Now Available

Always and Never: The Companion Journal

Self-reflection and the act of writing down your thoughts and observations can deliver greater awareness and joy to your life, helping you get unstuck and find new energy for taking action.

This journal will offer readers:
- An in-depth exploration of your relationship with media
- Exercises to disrupt mindless routines
- Reflection about habits that can sabotage your relationships and your own development
- A foundation for seizing control of your life and happiness
- Bonus section with a course outline and links to supplemental material for group study or retreats

If you would like to use this book and *The Companion Journal* in a group setting, visit www.lucidbooksbulk.com for bulk discounts.

For updates from Lisa, go to www.alwaysandneverbooks.com to sign up for her email list!